Flourish

Enjoying Life as the Pastor's Wife

Beverly Kimball

Cover Design: Joy McMillan

Edited by: Erin Brown

With love
to my husband,
David M. Kimball,
and to my family
who are my constant
cheerleaders,
sounding boards and
blessings.

Contents

Acknowledgments

Writing a book did not come easy to me nor was I able to do it on my own. Words cannot express all of the gratitude I have for my husband, who stood by my side and pushed me along to complete this journey. Along with my children, who each gave me such encouragement and showed so much excitement along the way. They gave me the drive to finish what I had started.

Special thanks also go out to my coach Darryll Stinson who gave me the kick I needed to take the steps of faith to go beyond my comfort zone and do what God had been prompting me to do for so long.

And finally, my editor, Erin Brown who lovingly pointed out the weaknesses, encouraged me in the strengths and was patient with my grammar. Your insights and thoughtful reading helped me say what I wanted to say in a much more professional manner.

Introduction

I've been a pastor's wife for twenty-six years. Although I am comfortable in my role now, I wasn't always. In fact, when my husband first proposed to me, I mentally ran through a checklist of my own devising that decidedly indicated I was not pastor wife material.

But let me back up a bit farther and tell you a little about a life-changing event.

When I was fourteen, my nineteen-year-old brother died in a motorcycle accident. I couldn't understand how God could let something like that happen. I blamed God and wouldn't believe He really loved me, for if He did, I wouldn't have to go through that loss. So I turned away from God.

To cope with the pain of losing my brother, I started looking for love in many places. I continued to put on my church face for youth group and church events, but my heart remained disconnected. I felt empty and lonely. I turned to comfort from people rather than from God. I began to flirt with any boy who was around. When I was with a guy, I felt special and happy for a moment when my pain seemed to subside, but I knew deep down that I was doing wrong. It wasn't long before the pain of loneliness returned. I experienced a nagging guilt about the choices I was making. Everything I did only added more pain to my life. I didn't know how to handle the pain in a constructive way.

Through the prayers of others, He never withheld His grace and love from me. God continued to call me and protect me. I have come to realize what could have happened to me and where I could have ended up, but, *praise* the *Lord*, His grace covered me even when I was unaware of my deep need.

Then, at a youth conference, I heard a speaker talk about how God loved me even through the painful times in my life. We live in a world of sin and imperfection; therefore, we will not live lives free from struggle, pain and loss, *but* God wants His relationship with us to be so close that we share our thoughts, feelings, and questions with Him even when we are angry or don't understand what's going on. I was seventeen and in dire need of that kind of relationship. I decided it was time to confide in Him, the One who truly loves me and wants the best for me. As I prayed that night, I told God all of my anger, confusion, and sadness. I did a little yelling at God, and He listened. I didn't feel condemned or shamed. I felt the weight of my guilt and anger lift, replaced with peace and love. I still didn't have all the answers I wanted, but I knew that I was in the care of someone who wanted me to feel loved and valued. It was the start of a journey of being the *real* me—the authentic person God had made me to be.

I offer this short testimony of my teenage years to demonstrate that pastors' wives are no different from public figures' wives, from CEOs' wives, from school teachers' wives—or any other wives. We are women who come from a variety of backgrounds, educational levels, and economic situations. In short, we are women with stories about how God revealed His love to us and saved us for all eternity. We may have different callings, but we are united in Him.

The first, maybe only, criteria for being a pastor's wife is to love God, glorify God, and serve God.

There is no "typical" pastor's wife, just as there are no "typical" pastors.

God created strong, hardworking women leaders as well as quiet, hardworking followers. When we see another pastor's wife who is different from us, it is not our place to say who is better suited for the position. Each church's needs are different, each husband is different, and each ministry is different. Until we as Christian women learn to respect one another and support one another, our position will always be easy to attack. Look at some of the different women in the Bible and what they were known for:

- Deborah: Confident Leader, Judge
- Miriam: Servant, Loyal, Courageous
- Ruth: Widow, Loyal, Committed
- Esther: Beautiful, Smart, Resourceful
- Jana: Witness, Bold
- Michal (Saul's Daughter): Courageous, Strong
- Priscilla: Worker, Evangelist, Resilient

Though I said that pastors' wives are not different from other wives, it is true that church members have certain expectations of their pastors' wives and families. Too many times the pastor's wife becomes a sounding board for congregants to air their grievances against the pastor. How do we handle obligations with which some churches burden us and our families? What actions can we take to allow our children to be children rather than PKs (preacher's kids) with all the accompanying unrealistic expectations? What can we do when the budget is shot but we're two weeks away from the next paycheck?

Sometimes being a pastor's wife is hard—really hard. I wish I'd had a pastor's wife to mentor me in my early married years, someone to help me navigate the occasional tumultuous waters of raising my family in a fishbowl life. With everyone looking on, sometimes judging the way I lived out my faith, the way I was a wife to their pastor and the way I raised my children.

That's what I hope this book you're reading is for you. I hope to encourage you in your role as Christian, wife, mother—oh yes, and pastor's wife. I humbly offer you my experiences as a pastor's wife.

Chapter 1

Who Am I?

After dating a young man for over a year, he sat me down on the couch one day and started talking about marriage. I immediately panicked. This young man was going into the ministry as a pastor. My image of a pastor's wife was the put-together woman who had her spiritual life all worked out and had it altogether. That was not me. My past was not perfect. I was a sinner who had lived to please myself and others, not God. I didn't have the "right" talents: playing the piano or working with children's church. Too often I spoke my mind before thinking about what I was saying. I could never be the kind of pastor's wife whose life would honor God.

My wise husband-to-be (I finally said, "Yes!") reminded me that my past was my past and that God had transformed me into a new creation. No "talents" were required to be the wife of a pastor, and I could continue to be the person God created me to be while growing in my faith, regardless of my spouse's career. My personality was a gift from God, and, as I matured, God would use it for His glory.

I grappled with these thoughts for quite a while until I was willing to understand who I was in Christ. I had to *know* and understand God's love for me, the trust He had in me to accomplish His purposes, and that He had created me with my unique personality for a reason.

So, who am I in Christ? I am created in God's image, and knowing Him gives me a clearer vision of His will for me and what he wants me to accomplish. He sees the potential in me and empowers me, through the Holy Spirit, to achieve His desires for my life. Therefore, I have come to understand how God sees me as I give my life to Him:

- I am forgiven
- I am loved
- I am unique
- I am free

- I was bought with a tremendous price
- I was created to praise God
- I was created in His image (I bear His image)
- I have a purpose
- I have a gift/talent God wants to use

God loves me. I still do not fully grasp the depth of God's love for me, but I have experienced in many ways how much he loves me. If you attended church as a youngster, you probably sang "Jesus loves me, this I know, for the Bible tells me so." I always had the head knowledge that Jesus loves me, but when it really reached my heart, He changed my life. Probably the biggest change was my false belief about love. I had always thought that love here on earth came from people. I searched for it and sometimes even thought I had found it. But I still felt empty. Something was missing. Once I was able to realize that true love only comes through Christ, I was humbled and amazed that He would choose me to be his friend. In His love I am satisfied.

In my early thirties, I struggled with witnessing. I felt inadequate and feared saying something wrong. I had been a pastor's wife for several years at this point, and my lack of witness embarrassed me.

Adrian Despres, a speaker at our district youth camp one year, caught my attention when he talked about using certain techniques when witnessing. He put us into pairs to "practice" on each other. I ended up being paired with him. Talk about intimidating! He asked me what my story was. I shared how God had reached out to me in my rebellion and how His grace and love finally took hold. Adrian then assured me that I don't have to have all the "right" answers before I talk with people about God. The Holy Spirit is with me and will guide my thoughts and my words. He also reminded me that I am not responsible to do God's part of salvation. My only responsibility is to share what Jesus is to me and how He wants to be the answer to a lost world—their decision is not on me. I am not in control of the responses of others, but I can control how I obey the Holy Spirit in my own life. This knowledge freed me.

God still shows me His love by helping me understand that I am part of God's plan for the world. He believes in me and will equip me to do my part well. We are each the hands and feet of Jesus. Each one of us has a part in glorifying God here on earth and bringing people to Jesus.

As I continue to learn who I am in Christ, I have found other tools that help me discover more about how I am knit together. Personality tests reveal some of our characteristics. Understanding the unique way God knit us together and how that ties together with the abilities and gifts He has given us helps us find our place in God's plan.

Three things I want you to remember from this chapter:

1.   Know who you are in Christ
2.   Know that God has a plan for you in the world
3.   It's okay to be yourself

You were created for here and now. Allow God to use you as you are, now. Stay authentic as you love the world around you.

We need to know how God has knit us together and what roles He has for us. We need to stop putting the position of pastor's wife in a box.

Chapter 2

Contentment

As new parents of a two-week-old baby, my husband and I took our first official position after college at a church in Jonesboro, Arkansas. We were young, excited, and scared at the same time. I didn't know how to care for a baby, let alone care for a baby in unfamiliar surroundings, with no family to support me, and no house to make a home for my little family.

Our first few months in Jonesboro, we lived with another couple, and their baby, who was pastoring at the church. About the same time, the other pastor's wife and I discovered we were both pregnant. Two pregnant women, two babies, one dog, and two husbands who were working to restart a church = a recipe for stress.

My husband and I searched for quite a while to find a house to rent. It was an old shotgun style house located next to the railroad tracks. The living room became the baby room and our bedroom was everything else. We stayed there for only six months and then moved into our final home in Arkansas, located in the "rough" part of town.

I was excited to meet the neighbors and spread the love of God throughout the area. During the first week in our home, one of the neighbors came over and introduced herself. We had a nice talk. Before leaving she asked if she could borrow our vacuum cleaner, as hers had broken the week before. I was eager to help this "lost soul," so I agreed and even helped her get it out to the sidewalk. A few days later, her mother stopped by, who also lived in the neighborhood. We chatted awhile. She asked me if I had loaned anything to her daughter since moving in, so I told her about the vacuum. She hung her head and said, "Please, do not lend her anything else. I am sure she pawned your vacuum cleaner for drug money."

Well, that burst my evangelism bubble. We chatted a little more and then she left.

My frustration grew as I considered what she'd told me about her daughter selling my vacuum cleaner. Why did my good deed have to cost me? Then God, in His loving way, reminded me that the cost of a vacuum is little compared with the cost of a relationship. I never saw my vacuum again but continued to build relationships in the community, although with more discernment. I learned that generosity is part of being a Christian. It doesn't matter if things go as I had planned, God can use any opportunity to help me see needs and hurts around me.

Our home was not only in the rough part of town, but being in the South I had an ongoing battle with roaches. If you have ever lived in the South, you know the struggle. They were everywhere. We called in the local bug exterminator company. For the entire year and a half we lived there, the exterminators came twice a month to treat our home, but the roaches, hearty insects that they are, never retreated. I had to wash our dishes *before* we ate, and I never felt like I my home was ever totally clean. To this day, the roach invasion has been the worst experience in any of our homes.

We lived in several different places throughout the next twenty years of ministry. One home had a basement. But I had to wear waders to get to the washer and dryer, which sat on cement blocks. They were raised so high off the ground that I could hardly reach down to the bottom of the washer. This one-bedroom home housed us and our four children. Two kids took the bedroom, two kids were on the landing at the top of the stairs, and my husband and I slept in the office, which was really just a bedroom, as our queen size bed was all that would fit in the room. We kept our dressers and clothes in the living room.

I love to entertain, but you can imagine it was somewhat embarrassing to have our dressers as our entertainment center and our clothes hanging on a wall. Frustration became my constant companion. In all the places we had lived over the previous ten years, none was conducive to having people over for a nice evening. We never had any room. Nevertheless, we made the limited space work. We always hosted Bible studies and had friends over for dinner. I had to learn that people don't look at things the way I do. They want relationships not perfect homes.

But we have lived in wonderful houses too: a four bedroom, full basement home on two acres of land, and a beautiful home next to a country club. But I discovered that none of those houses made my life better or worse. While living in each home, we had times of growth; made precious family remembrances; and experienced rough, painful encounters. God worked in our lives and we have special memories of His love and grace at each place we have lived.

As Paul said "I know what it is to be in need, and I know what it is to have plenty. I have learned the secret of being content in any and every situation, whether well fed or hungry, whether living in plenty or in want" (Phil. 4:12). I agree that it is not the things I have that create peace and joy in my life. It is my response to my circumstances and my ability to see what God wants to do through each circumstance. My peace and joy are seated in God's faithfulness and trustworthiness. Though locations and housing conditions may change, God remains unchanging.

In our second home in Arkansas, my brother visited to see how his little sister was doing. A line dance instructor in Michigan, he went to a club by us to see what the newest steps were. There he met a girl, who later became his wife. Long story short, this incident brought him back to church. To this day, his family is a strong Christian family. My point? At that time we were living in the shotgun, roach-infested house, but God used that situation as an opportunity to bring about His will in my brother's life, and eventually in his family's life.

Through all these times and places, I learned the joy found in being content.

Another area that causes us to be discontent is our finances. Our financial situation determines the amount of money available for housing, transportation, food, and clothing. It is the first thing we have to come to terms with as we work with whatever amount of money God provides for our family. Contentment is a key aspect of financial freedom.

I had to come to terms with financial management as I learned contentment. Truth be told, I am still learning how to make godly financial decisions, and I confess that I have not been good at budgeting, saving, and applying God's financial principles in my life. But as I learn and make better decisions in this area, I'm also becoming a more content Christian, wife, and mother.

Using a godly financial planner to assess our financial habits, my husband and I are focused on managing wisely and efficiently what God provides. The more we align our financial lives with God's way, the more He can do in and through us.

Maybe you struggle with finances. Possibly you believe if you had more money, you'd be more content. Let me share some key principles of finances I have learned through the years, which has contributed to my contentment:

- Stay out of debt (See Proverbs 22:7; Romans 13:8)
- God knows your needs and will provide; be patient
- Be wise with what God has given you; budget and learn how to save
- Be generous as God leads; be a giver

Though I have not mastered these financial principles—God's principles—when I follow them, God blesses in many different ways:

- my boys' clothes last way longer than they should have
- the gas prices go down just when needed

- a kind friend leaves a bag of groceries on our steps at just the right moment
- and the list goes on and on

When I follow God's principles in my finances, my trust in His faithfulness increases, as does my contentment.

The heart of contentment, living debt free, is countercultural. It means, at least for a time, we don't do big vacations: Disney World, cruises, and resorts. It usually meant camping in our tents for vacations, finding free things to do in the towns around the campground or just enjoying the water close by. It means fewer meals at restaurants, and renting new releases instead of visiting expensive movie theaters. It means driving an older car instead of trading up every couple of years. It means not buying the latest techy device, which will be outdated within six months to a year.

Through our years of marriage, my husband and I have remained debt free. I won't deny that it was at times difficult, but it has served us well. Probably our hardest lesson regarding living debt free was early in our marriage and my husband's career.

Right out of college we bought a brand-new car, but after moving to Arkansas, we couldn't afford to continue the high payments. The value of the car was less than what we owed. We had to get out from under the payments. We humbly had to accept help from family to trade cars with one that wasn't as reliable, new, and shiny. Since then, we have relied on cash to buy used cars. God has always provided the money to buy a car when we needed it, and, a few times, people gave us a car when we didn't have the money. When we patiently waited on God to provide, He always did. We went many months with only one family car while we had four drivers in the home, all needing to get to different places. But as we prayed and waited, God provided.

Our children never lacked clothing. God allowed pants to somehow fit longer than they should have. He allowed shoes to last longer than I have ever seen (if you have kids, you know they grow out of new shoes in a matter of weeks!), and He always led me to the right garage sales or people whose child was just a little bit older than my own. My children never had the latest name-brand clothing, but they were well-dressed and good looking. I also taught our children that when we are able to provide for others, we paid that blessing forward.

The idea that more money equals more contentment is alive in some churches. I have heard this often: "If our church had more money, we would be able to do so much more outreach." And I've heard Christians say, "If I had more money, I could give more money to the ministry or charity." I believe the question we should be asking is, "Am I being responsible with what God has already given me?"

God did not intend for us to worry about finances. He promised that He *will* provide our *needs*. If we are seeking God's will first for our lives, we do not need to worry about what we will eat or what we will wear.

In our years of ministry, God has blessed us by way of other people meeting our needs. He has placed us in the right place to receive an answer to prayer. One instance that comes to mind was as we were moving to a new church in Owosso, Michigan. The men in the congregation came to help us unload the moving truck. They came back later in the day with a brand-new refrigerator because they had seen the rough shape of the one we moved.

People blessing people is one way God moves in this world. God knows *everything* about our lives and knows when we have a need even before we ask. Trusting in Him and knowing that He will do what He has promised is the first step toward financial stability.

Not only does God provide our needs, but sometimes He gives beyond the necessities and spills over into the extras. Again, I cannot tell you how many times God has blessed us above and beyond our needs. Our children are all very musical, and we could never afford all the musical instruments and training God has generously provided them. Things have "fallen into our lap" that can only be from God. How many people have had a marimba given to them? Or had a stranger offer to trade an amazing drum set for a rusty old truck? God knew that our kids would use those gifts to build their musical skills and someday glorify Him with their talents. Our children are all doing that today, and it is truly a blessing to many people.

Then we need to ask ourselves, "How much is enough?" "Are we spending too much money in any area?" One of my convictions came one day as I counted how many purses I had. As a teacher, I always asked my class weird questions about myself that they would have to try to guess the answer. One day, I asked them how many purses I owned. I didn't have any idea. Some women have an obsession for shoes, or jewelry, or some other type of accessory. Mine was purses. I went home that night and counted them. Forty-five! Wow! Even I was shocked. Did I really buy all those? And why do I *still* drift toward the purses on the clearance rack? I can use only one at a time. I can get so caught up in materialism because our world encourages us to get the "right" look. Market campaigns intentionally tell us how we should look and what name brand is hot. And we too often buy into it. We must keep God's Word in our hearts and minds, and remember that whatever He gives us, He expects us to use wisely.

Contentment's Benefits

One of the benefits of having contentment is being at peace. I almost wrote "feeling at peace," but this peace is more than a feeling. Rather, this kind of peace becomes a part of us and seeps into the core of our being.

While we were living in our roach home in Arkansas, we received a distinct call from God to move to Warrenton, Missouri. We had been through the toughest two years of our spiritual lives but had grown tremendously as a couple and as children of God. We knew it was time to move into this opportunity at a church in Missouri to work with a great pastor and his wife.

We decided to take a vacation before the move and went camping with my in-laws for a week. We returned to our home to find a broken sliding door, our front door nailed shut, and much of our belongings gone. I felt invaded, frustrated, angry, and scared. Someone had gone through every part of our home and lives, and took many our belongings.

After the initial flow of emotions, we came to the understanding that the stolen things amounted to just stuff. We looked at each other and said, "Well, I guess we have less stuff to move." We were all safe and God was still in control. *Only* then could we have peace and move on with our lives.

How does peace permeate our lives thus leading to contentment?

- Peace comes when we have forgiven those who have harmed us (or stolen from us).
- Peace comes when we have asked forgiveness of those we have harmed.
- Peace comes when we have given our worries over to God.

Until peace becomes a part of us and we allow the Holy Spirit to be in control of our thoughts, we cannot live at peace with others.

The mind of sinful man is death, but the mind controlled by the Spirit is life and peace.

Romans 8:6

Chapter 3

Parenting

If you have ever been to a children's Christmas program, you know that every parent and grandparent in the room has their eyes glued on their little one. They are hoping and praying that the child remembers his or her part and does a good job. Funny things always happen, and usually one or two children steal the show.

In one of our churches, just after our Christmas program, a dear lady brought our children out in front of the stage and handed them each a gift from the church and instructed them to open them right then. The other children on stage awkwardly watched as our children each opened a present picked out especially for them. The church was striving to be a blessing to our children but had put them and the other children, as well as the audience, in an uncomfortable situation.

After the service, we pulled the ladies responsible aside, thanked them for blessing our children, but then asked that in the future it would be best to do that in a private setting. Not only did it put our kids in the spotlight as "special," it left the other children on stage feeling not special. The ladies had never thought of that and handled subsequent years appropriately.

My husband and I had to advocate for our children. We instituted several key ways of helping our PK (pastor's kids) children feel like "normal" kids. We went against the accepted system of how the pastor's family should be, but we did what was healthy for our kids, which, in turn, served to develop in them several character traits.

First, taking the time to explain what you are feeling as a parent or how your children feel in church situations is very important. Talk to the people making the decisions, and gently inform them if something is not handled correctly. Throughout our ministry, we have had to take a stand for our children, but we have never regretted it. Pastor's kids are just kids. Learning, discovering, and questioning as they grow, just like every other child. They need to be treated the same as every other child in the church.

Second, we prayed desperately for other Christian adults who could be involved in our teenagers' lives. When children start to question what they believe and why, it is not their parents they usually turn to. They are looking for answers *other* than those that come from Mom and Dad. It is not wrong for them to do this. In fact, I encouraged it with my children. If children don't have relationships with other adults, then their peers become their counsel—the blind leading the blind. I wanted to connect them with adults who would help them along their journey to vibrant Christian living, give wise counsel when needed, and direct them in the ways of the Lord. Having other Christian adults in my kids' lives supports not only my children but me as a parent. Think back to when you were struggling as a teen, and about who you went to for advice. It probably wasn't your parent. Spend time with God to discover who is able to help equip your children, then work these adults into their lives to benefit your childrens' growth and development.

The third thing that stands out to me that we did differently was requiring our children to attend only two church events a week. Sunday morning was a priority in our home. Even on vacation we found a church where we could worship. We taught our kids that corporate worship is a need God has built into us, so it's vital to make time for it. Beyond that we let them choose when to be involved. They did not have to attend every church event or be in church whenever my husband and I were. Our kids were involved in sports, drama, NHS, Odyssey of the Mind, key club, and a myriad of other community activities. Those were an important part of their lives as well.

Let me ask you this: How can we be God's witnesses in the world if we do everything at church? When community events conflicted with church activities, we allowed the children to choose between events. Not just any reason would do. They knew their schedule for church and youth group and had to make clear choices beforehand. It was not something they could commit to and then change their minds. We also emphasized following through on their commitments.

My adult children, one who is now a parent, pointed out to us that we taught them through not only our words but through example. We taught our kids not to gossip by never talking about church people in their presence. They didn't hear the problems or the struggles we were discussing. Therefore, they loved the church people tremendously with no reservations.

We taught them about the worldviews behind movies, TV shows, commercials, and books. We helped them think through the intended message and to see it through the lens of the Bible.

We praised their efforts instead of their outcomes. Whether they failed or succeeded, they knew we were proud of them for trying.

When disciplining, we worked to helped them understand that they had made a bad decision, and that they were not a bad person.

My husband and I also made sure that we were in agreement about matters before confronting a situation. Our kids saw a united front and knew they could not work one of us against the other.

Setting boundaries for our children is a way to show them we love them. Children need boundaries set with love and acceptance. How we explain our boundaries is key to how effective they are. Explanations vary with the age of the child. Very young children and adolescents do not have the capacity to understand the consequences of their actions. Therefore, boundaries need to be in place for their protection.

As they mature, your children will come to understand the importance of what you have put in place and why you have set it. But as children grow and begin to question your boundaries, plan your response ahead of time so that you don't fall back on, "Just because I said so." This will not fly with thoughtful teenagers. When our oldest started asking for a cell phone "because everyone had one," we had to make a decision about when would be the best time to bring that technology into their lives. My husband and I came to a conclusion that they would get a phone when they started driving. We let our son know that a phone was not a necessity. It came with a monthly price tag that added to our budget, and he had other ways to contact us in an emergency. (A side benefit that our kids actually noticed was that because they were "disconnected," they didn't get pulled into as much middle school drama.)

Teaching them how to be independent was something we did without even realizing it. One day one of my children came home from school. Their class had been on a field trip that day and had gone to McDonald's for lunch. My child was amazed that several of her friends were afraid to go up to the counter to place an order. The students had no confidence in talking with a stranger or making the decision on their own. We have always had our children tell the person behind the counter what they wanted. When they were old enough to understand, we would give them a choice of two or three things and then let them pick. When they could read the menu, we let them look it over and decide what they wanted. This is such a small example but one that stood out to *them*.

Every day I see students who don't know how to make simple decisions on their own. Independence will come, but will they be ready? We need to prepare them starting from the time they are born. It is hard to watch them fail sometimes, and it is hard to hold them accountable to their choices. But it is a life lesson that is much easier to learn with the little things and in a protected environment, so when they are faced with big decisions, they have the skills to make a wise decision.

Another skill that had helped me in parenting is knowing my child's personality and love language. Knowing what makes your child feel loved is a tremendous help, especially in their teen years. Each one of my four children have a different love language. If you have never read *The Five Love Languages* by Gary Chapman, be sure to check it out. The five are Words of Affirmation, Quality Time, Receiving Gifts, Acts of Service, and Physical Touch. When you know what works for your child, you save yourself a lot of heartache.

My daughter's love language is acts of service. She shows her love for me and my husband by washing the dishes, cleaning a room, or doing something nice for us. She also feels loved when we do something like that in return. If I help her clean and organize her room, she feels loved. She knows that I love her, but showing our love through acts of service speaks the most clearly to her. One of the boys has the language of physical touch. He loved to sit right next to me on the couch and read a book or play on his Gameboy. He just wanted to be in my space. That took some getting used to, but it was his language and I felt his love in that too. Find out what works for your child. You will usually see it first in the way they show love to you. Are they always making you a present, wanting to sit on your lap, seeking your approval or words of encouragement? These are signals that help us understand our children better.

Knowing their personalities is also helpful in understanding them and communicating with them. Many terms are used to label the different personality types, so find one you are comfortable with and figure out your children's personalities. Knowing if your child is strong-willed or compliant is easy to determine as they mature. But knowing the *root* of the strong will is another aspect of it, as is also the case with the compliant child. Knowing how your child is knit together is our job as parents. Once we see those things start to form and mature in our children, our job becomes steering that child in the right direction according to his or her personality. You can't make a shy, intelligent, reader-type student into the star of the school play just because you think she would be good. Instead, teach your children how to find things they are naturally good at, how they can excel in those areas, and how to use it for God's glory.

Chapter 4

Relationships

As I sit here writing tonight, I am on a "connection" trip with our church family. I was excited to get to know some of the women in the church better, but circumstances happened that left me the only adult woman on the trip.

As I was thinking through my relationships and the women in my church, I feel that the lack of creating close, long-lasting friendships is a common frustration among women. The friendships I mean are those in which you can talk about your struggles, your temptations, your insecurities . . . *everything*.

Writing from many years of experience of being in ministry in the church, I have concluded that Christian women struggle with self-esteem, self-confidence, and self-awareness just as much as non-Christian women do. We tend to put on a front so that we look good, are not perplexed by problems, or let on that life is less than perfect. We like to say all the "right" things when we are in small groups and never really challenge one another to go deeper. Why do we do this, and how do we build godly, deep relationships?

The "why" is different for many of us, but I think most struggle with either pride or insecurity. We don't want others to know our struggles or allow them to see us as weak or lacking in some areas of our lives. We don't want pity. We think we are protecting the Christian image by portraying "I have it all together" when really we are suffering in loneliness and feeling like we don't belong anywhere. People do eventually see through our façade, leaving us feeling like we can never be the good Christian woman we want to be. If you read the Bible, you know that it teaches the good, the bad, and the ugly about its characters. Are we willing to be authentic and real with the small group of close friends for the purpose of encouraging, supporting, and helping one another?

How do you find women who will connect with you? They have to be trustworthy and use biblical standards in sharing advice or encouragement with you. These women must be willing to put the time into the friendship. Close, meaningful relationships take time and energy. Once you have someone in mind, ask her. Don't be alarmed if she is surprised by your question. Ask her to think about it and prayerfully consider building that bond.

As if finding the relationship isn't hard enough, keeping this deep relationship can be an even tougher battle. If only one of the friends initiates every conversation and is the one who must go to the other's house to spend time together, problems are sure to pop up. Over my years of ministry, I have talked with several women who feel some of their closest friends always expect them to be the one to call or the one to come to their home. Some women quit calling a friend just to see if that person will initiate a call and then are offended if they do not connect. When we build relationships, we unknowingly have expectations for that friendship. Let me assure you that just because you are the one who always calls does not mean the other person doesn't value your friendship. She may feel it would be intrusive to call you because you are a busy person. Some people do not feel comfortable in other people's homes but love to have people in their home. Don't let unfulfilled expectations ruin a good friendship.

If you have expectations for a relationship, be sure to voice them. Discuss them with the other person and learn if these things are reasonable for both of you. If not, talk about and decide what does work.

I have typically been the "traveler" in my relationships. One of my closest friends has been to my home only once. If I start to feel that she doesn't love and appreciate our relationship because she doesn't come to my home, I am putting the value of our friendship on a place rather than on the person.

Satan loves to ruin relationships, and I have seen him use this tactic over and over again. He aims his attacks at our thoughts and assumptions. For example, "She doesn't think my home is good enough," "She never calls me; I always have to call her," "She isn't willing to take the time to make the trip," and on and on it goes. But those are rarely if ever the source of the problem; instead, it's our unstated expectations. If you find you're entertaining thoughts like these that are affecting your friendship, talk with her about it. Chances are very good that you will discover your friend loves and appreciates your friendship. She will likely be very sorry that her misstep hurt you and will want to make changes that strengthen and enrich the cherished friendship.

Additionally, we need close friends who can share in our struggles. Confessing our temptations and failures helps us to grow stronger; it cleanses the soul. It frees us from Satan's trap of thinking that if we hide it, it will go away. That is just one of his many lies. We need to voice our struggles and face whatever it takes—consequences, changes in lifestyle or thinking, etc.—to conquer that sin. How can you conquer an enemy you are trying to hide? Being open about our struggles encourages others with the same struggle to open up about them. Knowing we are not alone and that we need each other in this Christian life encourages and emboldens us to "run the race set before us."

Just this past year I sinned because of "my own evil desires." I gave into something I have not done in eighteen years. No one at my church would have known, my husband would not have known, so I could have easily hidden it. But I have struggled with this weakness, and even though it had been a long time since I slipped, I needed others to help me overcome this temptation. I did not get up in front of church and confess my sin; rather, I shared it with two ladies in the church and my husband. The relief I felt just sharing triggered the beginning of my conquering it. I will always have this weakness, but others holding me accountable and remembering how I have let God down kept me from giving in again.

Please find a few ladies you believe are trustworthy, mature Christians you can be open with and receive prayer from when you are struggling. As Jesus said, "In this world you *will* have trouble." And we need one another to help us in our walk with Christ.

Chapter 5

Stress

In our first ministry, I was a new mom, in a new community, and still working on figuring out what my role as a pastor's wife was supposed to look like. I still struggled with feeling inadequate. My self-talk sounded like this: "I don't know what I'm doing," "I can't play the piano," "Why is my child crying?" "Why can't I teach?" "People are going to think I'm *just* a stay-at-home mom," "I'm not contributing to my husband's ministry at all." *Stress.*

Also in that first ministry, we were dirt poor. My husband's church paycheck barely covered rent. He worked a minimum-wage job just to pay the other bills and feed us. In that first year we had another baby, and looking at the finances on paper was terrible! We couldn't possibly pay for everything we needed, and for me to go to work meant my paycheck would only pay for childcare, so my working outside the home was not sensible. *Stress.*

I have a dear friend who is a pastor's wife and struggled physically for two years. She was typically a go-getter, but getting out of bed sapped her waning energy. Doctors couldn't find anything wrong. *Stress.*

My current job involves working with troubled teenagers. I'm always faced with new problems, angry responses, and unpredictable behavior. Each day holds something new, and I'm not sure I'm ready to handle it properly. *Stress.*

For nine months we had the privilege of our son and his new family living with us. Having a toddler and a baby in the house again was so much fun, but I quickly became reacquainted with an unorganized home. Toys, diapers, and two families' worth of stuff that doesn't fit neatly into one home . . . it seemed I was constantly looking for something or trying to figure out where to put something. *Stress.*

Last year my dear, sweet, amazing husband surprised me with a hot tub. Boy, do I use it every night to de-stress!

Who doesn't want a stress-free life? Recently I was visiting some dear friends at the Cleveland Clinic. They shared something they had learned that I had never thought of before. While they were learning how to manage pain, their mentor asked them to write down the benefits and detriments of pain. At first, the thought of writing down any benefit seemed unusual, but the more they considered it, the more items they listed. Their benefits list became bigger than their detriments list.

Let's take that concept and apply it to stress. Is some stress good? How do we know which stress is good and which stress is bad? Let's write out some things.

Good stress can . . .

- motivate us
- help us focus and find ways to fix problems
- increase short-term adrenaline rushes to deal with crises
- provide suspense and excitement in our lives

Bad stress can . . .

- cause physical problems like lack of sleep, high blood pressure, and other chronic health issues
- immobilize us and keep us from moving forward

Some of the greatest moments in the life of our family produced stressful situations. Getting married, having a baby, moving, and taking the next steps in my career were all stressful times. For me, writing this book was stressful. The stressful situation is not going to go away without a response from us. What might that response be? We can use the stress to motivate us in some way to change either the situation or our thinking about it and, thus, move us forward. Or we can dwell on the stress and become exhausted, unfocused, and stagnant.

Prolonged stress needs to be handled entirely differently. Locating the source of the stress is the first step. Is it your thought life; finances; health issues; family, friends, or co-workers; lack of organization—as the opening stories illustrates—? Once you know the source, find ways to help you manage those things.

Let's take each of these common stress producers and discover how to de-stress them.

Listening to motivational speakers, reading self-help books, and studying Scripture helped my thought life. I had to learn to take every thought captive and determine if my thought was true or false. If the thought was false, I had to replace it with truth. If it was true I had to determine if it was something I could, or should, change. If I couldn't change it, I needed to leave it there.

Regarding our finances, I simply had trust in God. Yeah, *simply*. Who said it was simple, right? Those two years in Arkansas were my most faith-testing and faith-growing times I have ever experienced. God always provided. We never went hungry, though we ate a lot of rice and turkey, but we were fed. Our children always had diapers, food, shelter, and protection. We always had a vehicle that worked, although one would not go into reverse. On paper, we should not have survived those two years, *but God* provided. To this day, whenever I doubt, I always look at how God was my

Provider back then. And I remember He is still my Provider. We discovered some stewardship ideas in Chapter 2 "Contentment," but the first step to relieving stress concerning finances is to turn your needs over to God.

When it comes to our physical well-being, we need to remember that our physical bodies are connected to every other part of us. We need to pay attention to what our bodies are saying. My body tells me when it is hurting, exhausted, and needs rest and restoration. I need to heed these physical signs to also stay emotionally and spiritually healthy, otherwise stress will continue to build.

During the three years at my job as Alternative Education teacher, I could never be totally prepared for everything I encountered, but as I went through each struggle, I became more knowledgeable and equipped to handle it better the next time. Sometimes the stressful situations we face teach us how to deal with situations better and to listen to the Holy Spirit's promptings. Some days I didn't know where the patience and strength to keep quiet came from, but I knew that my days were covered in prayer and that God never left me. We can't always stay away from stressful people during our daily lives, but we can be sure to have a prayer covering by some faithful friends to keep us calm during these encounters. Prayer is essential to this, as is listening to the Holy Spirit when making quick decisions. If you develop the habit of listening during the quiet, still times, then you will learn to hear Him through all the noise as well.

As we go through situations that upset our normal routines, we have another thing that can cause stress . . . change. I am a Type A personality. I like to have a plan, a list, and know what and where things are. During the nine months when my oldest son and his family lived with me, I had to revert to some of the teachings I learned when I had toddlers of my own. The clean, organized home is not as important as snuggling, reading, and holding the precious ones God has put in my care. On the other hand, we had to find creative ways to organize and put things away so that little hands could not find them. Problem solving and creativity come in handy during stressful situations. Use those skills to work through those times.

Another practice that helps in stressful situations is to praise God. God created us to praise! One Sunday morning our drummer talked to me after the worship part of the service. He said, "I didn't want to come today. It was cold, I didn't feel good, and I knew I had to leave church early to go to work, *but* I am so glad I came. What a blessing the worship was today!"

I know you have had moments when you do not *feel* like praising God, but once you do, the trials and troubles seem to disappear or lessen in significance. Praise is not about a feeling; rather, it is a choice we make. No matter where we are, what the circumstance is, or how we feel, it is always a good time to praise the Lord.

Think about Paul and Silas in prison (see Acts 16). Do you think they *felt* like praising God? But look at the outcome of their praise. They led the jailer and his whole family to the Lord. When we choose to worship, God uses our praise to reveal Himself to other people and He fills us with encouragement.

Do we all have bad days? Absolutely! But the life of a Christian is meant to be a blessed and wonderful life. Remember that Jesus said that is why he came. John 10:10 "… I have come that they may have life, and have it to the full." No matter what the circumstances, we need to find ways to give praise to God. How do we do that? Following are just four ways to get started:

1. Remember the price Jesus paid for your sin.

2. Find a song that you love and helps you focus on Christ. Sing at the top of your lungs; or listen to the song on one of your devices and focus on the words.

3. Read the Word! It is amazing how God's Word can feed us and bring us to a point of praise. Start with these great verses: Psalm 3:4, Isaiah 55:6, Psalm 146:5–6, and Ephesians 3:20–21.

4. Change your focus from the situation or problem to praise and gratitude for what God has done in the past or the blessing you see around you.

Praise has a way of changing our outlook on the circumstances we face. Practice it daily and watch your life change!

Chapter 6

Balance

For four years, my life was completely out of balance. I was teaching full time—seven different classes each day. My college courses had not prepared me for the amount of time I spent grading and planning for so many classes. The school also required me to do one extracurricular activity to support the school, so I was coaching a cheer team. We had practice three times a week and performed during the games twice a week. I also worked with my husband with the church youth group. That entailed meeting twice a week with teens, doing fun events with them, and being available as a mentor to the young ladies in the youth group. On top of that I had a three-year-old and a two-year-old. A year later I was pregnant again and gave birth to our third son during this time.

My husband was just as busy. We left home at 6 a.m. and typically didn't get back home until 10 p.m. Our kids were in day care from 7 a.m. to 5 p.m. and then we brought them with us as we did ministry.

We finally realized that our schedule was not allowing us to be the family God intended us to be. We had to take a drastic step of faith to change our circumstances.

Our lives will never be perfectly balanced because of the situations that are part of our lives. For example, a newborn baby in the home means something in the schedule has to give for the well-being of the baby. While being a parent's caregiver, life will likely become unbalanced. Indisputably, we must keep the important things to the forefront and the time-wasting things to the side. And often the decision as to what is important and what isn't might not seem black-and-white.

I loved all the things I was doing. I enjoyed working with teens, and my heart will always be with them. They were a great group of kids who were thriving and growing in Christ. Teaching brings me great joy and I relished stretching the minds of those high school students. Ministry is vital to my life and my husband's, but our responsibility as parents had to come first. As a mother, I was to teach my children about God's love and be an example to them. I needed to be healthy and spiritually strong to do that, but both of those areas were suffering during those four years. Additionally, my husband and I had no time for romance and building our relationship. We didn't have a Sabbath or day of rest in our schedule because we were so involved in the church. Furthermore, we were also feeling the pull of extended-family relationships. Both of our families lived several hours away, and we were missing that support system.

As we determined and implemented necessary changes, my husband and I made our relationship a high priority, and we were purposeful as we crafted meaningful time with our children. Strong relationships don't develop by accident. They require conscious effort. The balance between God, family, church, and community is vital to effective ministry. We will have seasons where that balance is off, but when we see that happening, we look for ways to bring it back into balance. Our witness is not only what we do in our ministry, but also how we develop our marriage and family.

When the New Testament church was looking for elders, they specifically wanted those whose families were strong, healthy, and intact.

Sometimes our lives are so far out of balance for many years that we don't even recognize what a balanced life looks like. Let me offer some ideas my husband and I have used. We don't always do these things, and some are not always feasible, depending on the point in our journey. But overall, this is what we have found helps to keep us focused.

1. Date Nights

Plan regular date nights with your spouse. During several years of our ministry, lack of excess money did not allow for "lavish" dates (dinner and a movie), so sometimes we picnicked at the park or just window shopped in the neighboring city. Think about the many ways you can spend time alone together without spending any money.

2. Cultivate Friendships

Valuable friendships add so much to our lives. Make time for those top ten friends whose input you value. Schedule times for coffee or phone calls. Keep connected to those who can keep your life focused and on track. (See the Chapter 4 "Relationships" for more information.)

3. Be Grateful

Make time for gratitude. Be thankful for the little things God does and provides. Be thankful for the people who come in and out of your life, bringing sunshine and hope. Be thankful for the family of God that is supportive and compassionate. Find ways to show your gratitude and let others know what you are specifically thankful for. Please don't just say, "Thank you for blessing me." Be specific. "Thank you for calling at just the right moment," or "Thank you for sharing your journey with me so I can see how God is working around me." Let people know when they are a blessing to you.

4. Have a Hobby

You may have seasons of life when it's not possible to engage in a hobby. But remember, it's just a season not your whole life, so hang on to that hobby you enjoy. God gives us gifts and talents in many ways, and a hobby is one way of using a gift God has given you. Hobbies allow you to be creative and thoughtful.

5. Say No to Church

It is okay to be too tired to attend something at church. You are not super woman, and you can't do everything. If church activities take up three nights a week, pick and choose which one(s) to be involved in. I hope we do not expect every church member to be involved in everything that goes on at the church, and we should not have that expectation of ourselves. Be sure to know where you are effective and where your gifts and talents would best be used to serve the church, but don't think you must do everything.

6. Have Fun!

The proverb is true: All work and no play makes Jane a dull girl. It's up to you to make sure your life isn't one busy task after another. Your calendar is not a dictator to you; rather, you should be controlling your calendar. Have some fun with life, with your family, with your church, and with your friends. God wants us to enjoy our time here on earth, and we know that laughter is great medicine. So enjoy things along the journey!

Chapter 7

Confidence

While growing up, I was painfully insecure. My hair was too curly, I was overweight, I wasn't good enough on the team or in the choir . . . at least I told myself these things.

My goal in high school was to please people. When I was at youth group, I was a great "Christian" kid. When I was with the tennis team, I was the sports nut. When I was with the guys, I was the flirt. I desired to be loved and appreciated, and the only way I knew how to make this happen was to play the part of what each group determined was cool.

Living this way marked me with exhaustion, confusion, and stress. I was never just me. In fact, I didn't even know who "me" was. I never thought to ask myself: What do I really enjoy? Which friends would like me if I was just me? Does it matter if everyone likes me? Where is my Christian faith showing up in this group? Truth be told, I didn't think. I was just living to please others and hoping to be accepted and loved.

By the time I was seventeen, I had done a great job messing up my life. I repented, and repented again, and then repented some more, but I never changed.

Then, at a youth conference, I caught a glimpse of how much God loved me. He loved me just as I was! Without all the superficial masks I wore. That was the beginning of seeing myself as God sees me and finding out who He created me to be.

Still, it took a long time to really understand this unconditional love and acceptance from my heavenly Father. Even after marrying, it took my husband several years of telling me I was beautiful. He even stood me before a mirror and said, "You are beautiful, Beverly," and then he'd name the beauty he saw in my eyes, my smile, my hair, my hands . . . It took many years of hearing my husband affirm me this way before I grasped that God had made me the way I am: unique and designed specifically for an amazing purpose. I was beautiful! I need only to recognize who I am in Christ.

I lived the life that unfolded before me because I wasn't looking for the plan God had laid out for me. I didn't know how to be strong, confident, and proud of who God made me to be. I struggled to find the confidence that comes from hearing God's voice and knowing I can do what He asks me to do with His help.

I used to believe that confidence came from feeling "put together," knowing what my goals were, standing tall, and having "the walk." But then the Word of the Lord showed me that I needed to have inward confidence that only comes from trusting in Him and knowing who I am in Christ. As I studied Scripture and started to see myself through God's eyes, I realized I was called to be holy! If we are filled with the Holy Spirit, we are holy! Wow! I am holy! I am God's daughter. I know who I am, and no one can take that away from me. Do you know who you are in Christ? Do you act like you are God's daughter, holy to Him?

As I learned how God looks at me, I started to see that he doesn't love me because of the things I have or have not done. He loves me and wants to be in a relationship with me because of His great mercy.

> But when the kindness and love of
> God our Savior appeared, he saved us,
> not because of righteous things we
> had done, but because of his mercy.
> He saved us through the washing of
> rebirth and renewal by the Holy
> Spirit, whom he poured out on us
> generously through Jesus Christ our
> Savior, so that, having been justified
> by his grace, we might become heirs
> having the hope of eternal life.
> (Titus 3:4–7)

I am who I am in Christ not because of anything I have done but what Christ has done in me. Therefore, I can have full confidence in knowing that the Holy Spirit is at work in me, making me into the person God called me to be. I have some part to play in making sure I am fully trusting in Him as my Lord and Savior and seeking His will. I need to fill my mind with His Word and continue to grow in my relationship with Him through worship and prayer.

As we continue to grow in our faith, God builds in us the ability to go into situations with confidence. When Jesus taught His disciples, He explained that they didn't need to worry about what was going to happen. Jesus assured His disciples, "Whenever you are arrested and brought to trial, do not worry beforehand about what to say. Just say whatever is given you at the time, for it is not you speaking, but the Holy Spirit" (Mark 13:11). We, too, can be confident, knowing that the Holy Spirit will guide us in any circumstance. Be bold in the Lord and have confidence in who you are in Christ. That confidence will carry out into every aspect of your being.

Many women struggle to find balance between confidence and pride. I think the word *pride* is our stumbling block. We know the verse "pride goes before destruction" (Prov. 16:18a), but in studying this portion of Scripture, I do not think this means the kind of pride we take in our God-given strengths and gifts. I believe the second part of that verse conveys the heart issue we need to be worried about: "a haughty spirit before a fall" (v. 18b). Haughtiness means to feel superior and to have an arrogant attitude. That type of heart will lead you astray, but the pride that comes in being confident in who we are in Christ's helps us move forward in carrying out God's will for us. We are world changers, and we need to have confidence in our ability to let God use our strengths and weaknesses to further His kingdom.

For the past five years, God has been calling me to write a book. Who? Me? I came up with numerous excuses why not to write a book. I found many good things to keep me busy, and I practiced creative avoidance each and every chance I had time to write.

I actually argued with God! "I'm a math teacher not an English teacher. I have never been good at spelling. My thoughts aren't important to others. I am too busy . . ." And the list of excuses went on and on.

My brain is wired to justify my actions and decisions. That is true for most of us. Have you ever done something wrong and knew it was wrong, but right away you came up with a good reason you did it? Or maybe you wanted something that you didn't need or wasn't particularly good for you, but that great brain of yours thought of a reason to justify the want. Human nature makes us that way. It is a way of protecting ourselves and making us feel "right." However, if we listen to that nature, our morality will easily get ensnared in sin.

Besides making excuses and finding logical reasons for not writing, I found other things to do and made them sound important—pressing, even. I started a new business to help women. I met amazing people through that journey and shared my faith along the way. I made money, friends, and influenced some of the ladies in my circle. It was a good thing to do. *But* it wasn't what God had asked me to do. I had found something else I enjoyed doing to keep me from doing the scary thing God was asking me to do. I wanted to stay in my comfort zone, and God wanted me to step out of it.

I practiced creative avoidance in that when my scheduled time to write arrived, suddenly the dishes had to be done, the laundry needed to be folded, vacuuming became a priority. I would find any activity I thought was "necessary" to fill my time instead of doing what I knew was my calling. I can be very creative in devising ways to avoid the uncomfortable. How about you?

Jonah did it. He didn't want to go to Nineveh and found a boat that was sailing in the opposite direction. Moses did it. He believed he didn't have the right speaking voice, so God provided Aaron. But if you read through the rest of the stories, Jonah landed in Nineveh and preached to the citizens, and Moses ended up doing most of the talking anyway. The Bible is full of people who did not want to step out and do what God called them to do; but, in the end, God used them in mighty ways. We all will come to a point in our lives when we must decide: "Am I going to do something, or am I going to do *the* something?"

As you discover what God wants you to do, you need to know your strengths and weaknesses. Do you know what tempts you? Do you know what areas of your life are the most vulnerable? Do you know what you are good at? Have you taken a life inventory and understand how you are put together? The more you know about yourself, the greater your confidence to say no when necessary and to say yes when it's right. Don't be the person who agrees to fill every position because "someone has to do it." It might be appropriate to step in temporarily, but just because something needs to be done does not mean you are the one who must do it.

My schooling and practicums have taught me that working with small children is not my cup of tea. I can teach a lesson now and then, but to regularly be responsible for nursery or elementary age children is not for me. I have the confidence that if no one wants to work in the church nursery, our congregation must be okay with having babies in the worship service. If someone is sick one Sunday, I most definitely will fill in, but I understand enough about myself to know that this is not where God intends me to be every week. He has someone in the body for that position, and if others step into this position out of some sense of duty, God's choice may never have the courage to step up and accept his or her position in the body. It is acceptable to let a program in the church die rather than take it upon yourself to run it if it is not your calling. If you're too busy filling the position that you don't like and aren't good at it, you run the risk of missing out on the calling God has specifically made you for. *You will miss out on the joy of living out your faith.*

Chapter 8

Spouse/Marriage

Your marriage is the most important relationship you need to keep strong, healthy, and godly. Jesus used marriage as an example of His relationship to the church. That is how important he views marriage. The condition of our marriages affects our children, our extended families, our churches, our communities, and all the way to our country and beyond.

People whom I barely know ask me how my husband and I are still so happy after such a long marriage (twenty-eight years as of this writing). Over the years I have seen common mistakes pastors' wives repeatedly make. My intent is not to point a finger but to help you learn how to build a healthy and happy marriage.

Publicly Complaining about Your Husband

As a young pastor's wife, I craved time with other women to learn how to navigate this new adventure with my husband, new church, and children. I had very good friends who were also pastors' wives, and when we would get together, it became a complaining fest. We all found it so easy to talk about the things our husbands did that frustrated us, disappointed us, or just plain drove us crazy. I believe Satan deceives us into talking about the negatives rather than focusing on growth and the future. When my husband does something that frustrates me, it is a natural urge to find someone to offer sympathy—another wife who deals with the same frustration.

And it wasn't just pastors' wives who engaged in complaining fests. In my experience, it seemed that whenever a group of ladies would gather, eventually the talk turned to gripes about husbands. And I have to admit that I laughed at television sitcoms that showed women spouting grievances against their husbands. In essence, I agreed with their demeaning comments.

But then God's Word rocked my world. I learned at a women's retreat to read the Bible until something spoke to me. Whether that is a couple verses or a couple chapters, I always know that God will speak to me through His Word if I take the time to read and listen for His voice. During one of those reads, I came to Proverbs 14:1 "The wise woman builds her house, but with her own hand the foolish one tears hers down." As clear as could be, I heard God tell me to replace the word *hand* with *words.* "With her own *words* the foolish one tears hers down." Wow! Was I building up my marriage with my words or tearing it down? Even though my husband didn't hear what I was saying, just by repeating my frustrations over and over, they stayed fresh in my mind and built up to something much bigger than just leaving his clothes on the floor.

I need to be so very careful about what I say about my husband to other people. Sure, I need to have an accountability partner who helps me when I am struggling in some way, but my public words should always build up my husband. Instead of trying to outdo one another on who has the most frustrating husband, I want the world to know the amazing things my husband does for me to show me that he loves me. I want my focus to be on how I know he cares for me.

Anyone we live with will have annoying habits, frustrating days, and will disappoint us at some point, but if we focus only on those aspects of the relationship, they are magnified, becoming the very thing that tears apart the relationship. "If you can't say something nice, don't say anything at all" must be applied when talking about the most important man in my life.

I Didn't Sign Up for This

Many pastors' wives reveal their struggle when they utter, "I never chose to be a pastor's wife." It is usually delivered with disdain and frustration. When a woman says this to me, I ask, "Before marrying their husbands, do most women know how their husband's jobs will affect their marriages?"

Many pastors we have befriended are second-career pastors. Their spouses probably never considered being a pastor's wife. Many people in our culture will change their career at least once in their lives. Your husband may be one of those who changed careers. Or maybe you knew he was going to be a pastor but you didn't know what all his job would mean for you. Now what? What does being a pastor's wife really mean?

In the next chapter "Boundaries," I will write more about this subject, but for now, I just want to challenge you to remember why you chose your husband. Every wife is affected in some way or another concerning her husband's career. Whether your husband is a doctor, lawyer, psychologist, store owner, politician, or any of a thousand other positions, some responsibility of some sort will fall on you as the wife. I have a friend whose husband is a truck driver. He is gone Monday through Friday every week, and is home only on the weekends. Oh, the challenges they face! But they face it together and have devised a system that works for the good of their relationship.

We married our husbands, hopefully, because we loved him and knew we wanted to spend the rest of our lives together. Then we made a covenant before God that we would be together through good times and bad. Choosing to be a pastor's wife was simply choosing to support my husband in his work and then carry out what God called me to do for Him in my work or home life.

I mentioned in previous chapters challenges we've faced. Satan's goal is break relationships. He will accomplish that goal if we let those challenges and our expectations destroy our marriages. Let's deliver a devastating blow to him by continuing to support our husbands and focus on what God would have us do as wives who love the Lord.

I Have a Headache

Withholding sex or using it to manipulate your husband will render a powerful effect on his emotional and sexual well-being. When we do not satisfy that part of our marriage covenant, it can be damaging. I learned early in our marriage that Satan uses this even more than finances to tear marriages and men's purity apart. First Corinthians 7:5 says, "Do not deprive each other except perhaps by mutual consent and for a time, so that you may devote yourselves to prayer. Then come together again so that Satan will not tempt you because of your lack of self-control."

Ladies, we *must* satisfy our husbands sexually. God made us to be one with our husbands. Communication is necessary in finding ways to meet his needs. Talk with him about your likes and dislikes, and learn what he likes and dislikes. Know your spouse's love language (*The Five Love Languages* by Gary Chapman) so that you can *show* him love in meaningful ways throughout the day. Foreplay and have some fun. Be willing to initiate physical contact throughout the day. Sex was not meant to be a burden or to be just endured. If you read Genesis 2:24–25, God desires us to be one as husband and wife. It is unhealthy not to want that in your marriage. Read the Song of Solomon together as a couple. It is in the Bible for a reason. If you struggle with this area, please seek biblical guidance and perhaps even professional counsel. Sexual fulfillment will change your marriage.

Last year I wrote a blog about what we as Christian women could do for our husbands on Valentine's Day. Here is the blog post:

We all know that Valentine's Day is for those who are in love. When we look at the Bible and see how God intended marriage to be, it is full of romance, respect, and sex. Yes, we need to talk about sex as Christian married women. Our husbands need to feel loved, respected, and sexy. It is all wrapped up in who they are as men. Valentine's Day is not *all* about women getting chocolate, dinner out, and romantic cards. Many women have expectations and complain if it is not like the commercials portray it to be. So here are some things you can do to make this day incredible for *him:*

1. Build him up in front of his friends. Let the people you hang around know something great your husband did for you or your family.

2. Tell him what you like. Don't try to be subliminal and leave him to figure it out. Let him know what you like and he will be truly grateful.

3. Lay out sexy lingerie on the bed so when he comes home he knows you were thinking about him and ready for a fun night.

4. Post an affirmation on social media telling the world that you love your man!

5. Dress sexy under your clothing. Be sure your husband sees what you are wearing underneath. I know we want to be modest and appropriate on the outside, but make your husband think about you all day.

6. Touch him as much as you can throughout the day. If he is not a touchy guy, then build him up through your talk. It's okay to talk sexy to your husband throughout the day, even if through text or email (make sure it is not company email or phone . . . Oops!)

7. Play a game of your choice in which loser loses an article of clothing (strip Uno, lol?).

8. Ask him what he likes you to do for him when making love.

9. Give him a massage.

10. Sex. Yes! That is how many men really want the night to end :)

As a pastor's wife, I have seen many women use sex as a tool to manipulate their husbands. That is not what God intended. It is to be mutually enjoyed and respected in every marriage. Do not hold back or hold out on your husband. Keep him thinking of you and you will be amazed at how he will make you feel.

We're Not Mind Readers

This leads us right into an all too common struggle in marriage: communication. You and your husband are made in unique ways; therefore, you both are different in many ways. We need to be open and honest with each other and quit expecting our spouses to somehow automatically know what we want or expect. Talk about your expectations. Talk about how you will handle discipline with the kids, talk about your sex life, talk about finances, talk about spiritual things. I know we blame the men a lot for not talking or not listening, but I also know that in a lot of my history I wasn't sharing anything meaningful either. If something is important to me, then it is my responsibility to communicate it to my husband. To expect him to somehow know, to read my mind, is unrealistic. Do whatever it takes to help him understand whatever you need him to know.

Chapter 9

Boundaries

As a pastor's wife, I have heard repeatedly the analogy of how I live in a fishbowl. People are watching me and my family. They tend to share their thoughts on what they see, no matter what our relationship might be. My family is an example to those around us, and it's up to us whether that example is good or bad. We must evaluate carefully what people say to us. Instead of immediately taking the offensive, I take a moment to think about what they said. I judge it to determine if it is truth. I must decide whether or not it is something in my control. And if not, let it go.

After a Sunday morning service, a member from our church asked me, "Why do you allow your teenage daughter to play on her phone during the message?" My daughter had not been sitting with me, so I was not sure what had transpired. My children know they are not to use their phones in inappropriate ways, so I said, "Thank you for your concern. I will talk with my daughter and find out about what was going on."

I could have fumed that this woman had singled out my daughter when I could picture all the other people in the congregation who were doing something other than listening to the sermon. And I could have pointed out to her that my daughter was probably not the only one messing with her phone. But what would that have accomplished?

When we got home, I asked my daughter if she had been on her phone during the service. I did not accuse her or reveal the name of the person who questioned it. She looked surprised that I would ask and replied, "Yes, my phone has my Bible on it and I was taking notes."

Awesome! We continued to chat about what she had gotten out of the message and had a wonderful talk about her thoughts.

I had a choice to make. Part of me wanted to call the church member and "set things right," but I was also thankful that people are concerned about my children, spoke to me about it, which led to a positive moment with my daughter. I waited until the next Sunday and told the member that as technology changes, more people will be using Bible apps on their phones, and my daughter could show her how to do this if she would like.

In Chapter 3 "Parenting," we touched on boundaries with our children. We make sure our children can be children. Though PKs, they will make mistakes and fall into temptation like most kids do, and they must learn like all children learn. There is nothing "special" about them except that I love them unconditionally, and the church is part of our family. My husband and I did not discuss church issues in front of our children *ever*! We helped them develop close relationships with strong believers, and did not get offended if they wanted to talk to them instead of us about certain issues. They were expected to attend church but were not required to do more than was expected from any other child or teen.

People are going to have all kinds of advice about the pastor's children, thoughts and judgments about our families. What pastors and wives need to remember is that our children need protection, positive adult interaction in the church, and people they can go to when they are questioning God, the Bible, life, and their parents.

My husband and I have boundaries as well. We have made a commitment not to put ourselves in situations that could cause problems within our relationship. I will not meet with a gentleman on my own, and my husband will not meet with a woman on his own. We will not give a teen a ride in the car by ourselves, and we will be sure not to have a Bible study/discipleship relationship with someone of the opposite sex. These are all protections we set very early in our marriage. Too many times I have seen emotional attachments lead to broken relationships. Families and churches have suffered because leaders put themselves in compromising situations. Be sure to sit down with your husband and set out what your parameters will be.

My husband also has boundaries with the congregation to protect me. I do not need to know everything that happens in a board meeting or in his discussions with board members. He has a discerning heart that lets me know what I need to know and protects me from other information. My husband has set this boundary to help me maintain healthy relationships in the church. If I think I should know every detail that goes on, it can possibly limit my effectiveness in relationship building. I don't have any business knowing what people give, what petty complaints people have about my husband, and what things board members discussed in their meetings. My husband lets the leaders know that he doesn't share everything with me, so a level of confidentiality remains between them.

I am a partner with my husband and support him as he leads, but that doesn't mean I am a church co-leader. I am an encourager, supporter, and prayer warrior. The church did not hire me. They called my husband as their leader. The congregation needs to understand what that means for them, and I need to understand what that means for me. The congregation must know that I am not the one who will fill all the empty positions in the church programs. I am not the one they call when they have a problem or an issue with my husband. I am not the complaint department. I am very thankful that my husband sets those boundaries when he is first hired in a position. He sets those boundaries so that all parties understand them.

Likewise, I need to know where to direct people when they call to discuss church-related issues. I need to know what I should listen to and what I should not listen to. I need to do the ministry I am equipped for and leave the other ministries to someone else. If no one else is available, maybe that ministry is to be put on hold for a while. We have gone without children's church for periods of time until someone steps up who has that gift. God can and will fill it if it will advance His kingdom.

Now, to get down to the nitty gritty. Ladies, we need to let our husbands lead. I am a leader. It is one of my spiritual gifts and shows up in my personality. But the church did not hire me to lead. Too many pastors' wives try to take over situations that arise in the church instead of letting their husbands handle it. You will be amazed at how God will use your husband's natural gifts and abilities in the church God called him to lead. God knew your husband *and* He knew the congregation. He created the perfect fit when He brought them together, but we wives have to let that happen. Let your husband lead and you be the strength and support he needs behind the scenes. If you want to be in leadership, go through the right steps and training to get ordained, to be the lead pastor, or to work alongside your husband as co-leader in the church. But if this is not your official position, don't take it over. Let the leaders God has put in place carry out their roles.

Afterword

As you can see, there are many people, situations, and events that try to steal our joy as pastors' wives. But as you work through life, God's desire is that our relationship with Him is the steadfast love that turns our trials into lessons and growth.

This book is a synopsis of some of the things I have learned over our years in ministry. As I prepare to publish I realize that I could probably fill a book for each chapter cover in this first book. I may begin writing more so let me know which chapter spoke to you the most.

Some amazing things have happened along our twenty-six- year ministry journey. We have been blessed with wonderful friendships in almost every state and several countries. With each relationship, we could connect and spend time with them at a moment's notice.

Also, whenever we have moved to a new town, (six major moves, four different states), our church family is instantly there to befriend us, share with us the ins and outs of the town, and help us in ways most families do not have when moving to a strange city. That is a huge blessing if you have ever moved to a town where you knew no one.

Another blessing is the way churches have enriched our family. Our children have received free music lessons from members of the praise team, who encouraged the kids to become better on their own. They learned to feel confident in front of an audience and were capable of interacting with adults. Our church families helped raise our children into the amazing, godly adults they are today. Praise God for people who were examples to our kids by truly loving God and others.

I am beyond blessed to be a pastor's wife, and I hope you feel the same way. David summed it up well in 2 Samuel 7:18: "Then King David went in and sat before the Lord, and he said: 'Who am I, Sovereign Lord, and what is my family, that you have brought me this far?'"

About the Author

My husband and I have been married twenty-eight years this summer. We have been in ministry twenty-six of those. I have a B.S. in Secondary Mathematics Education from Oklahoma Wesleyan University and am currently a certified teacher in Michigan. We have four amazing children, each one born in a different state, two awesome daughters-in-law (the third one joins our family in December 2017), and two outstanding grandsons.

I have held many jobs over my years as a pastor's wife, and God has used them all to shape who I am today. I have been a teacher, a store clerk, an office manager, a librarian, a stay-at-home and homeschool mom, a business owner, and now I add writer to this list. God has used me beside my husband throughout all those positions, and I know each one was placed at the right time.

I love camping, playing Pokémon Go, singing, and loving on my family. I am truly blessed by God and hope to continue in His mission for the rest of my life.